SEVEN WAYS TO HELP YOUR CHILD WITH READING

Dc

CONTENTS

Dear Parents,

Your role in helping your child to read is sometimes underestimated. There has been a policy of 'leave it to the experts', kindled by some teachers wary of 'interference', and fuelled by some parents afraid of 'doing the wrong thing'. So, learning to read has often been shrouded in a cloak of mystery and/or apprehension.

The big advantage that you as parents have in helping your child to read is that you have a better opportunity to show him how reading is related to everyday life and not just something that you do at school. You are also more easily able to provide an intimate, relaxed situation where you can give more individual time and attention than a teacher with a class of maybe thirty children could manage.

The following ideas will, I hope, show you how you can help your child.

Many of the items in the games and booklist are obtainable from school suppliers who also deal with private customers.

Barbara Geere (Cert. Ed.)

The child is referred to as 'he' in order to avoid the awkward 'he/she'.

BY EXAMPLE
1

One of the best ways of helping your child to read is by example. A child is a great imitator so if you want to interest him in books and reading you must show him that you, yourself, read for purpose and enjoyment. If he sees you reading regularly then he will learn by your example: you are still a source of wisdom and authority at this age! He will then be more likely to regard reading as something important.

Start looking at books with him from a very early age. Rag books and board books are good for a tiny child; they won't suffer too much from impatient hands. Turning over the pages gives him the idea of how to use a book, and he will gradually begin to get the idea that the black shapes on the page, combinations of circles and lines, mean something and can be the key to pleasure and information.

Joining a library is useful and will establish a good habit and attitude towards books as he sees other people interested, and especially you.

WHAT'S THE POINT OF READING?
2

If you can answer this question, and help him to understand what reading is all about, helping him to see what the connection is between rows of shapes on the page and the everyday words we speak, and how useful and enjoyable this can be, then you have laid the foundation for reading.

We take it for granted that we can find out where we're going by reading signs or information sheets, that we can read the detail of goods in shops, not to mention finding a whole world of fact, thought and imagination through books and newspapers,

It seems obvious to us, but **the child has got to see the point of reading** before he has enough motivation to want to learn. **talk to him** — not at him — as you do the shopping, letting him see you use the large notices in supermarkets which indicate the position of different goods.

Look at the packets or labels for information.

Encourage him to look at the cereal packets at breakfast.

Look at the names of streets and roads, especially in a new area, showing him how you can use the names from a map to find your way. Look also at the names of shops. Railway stations have signs and notices giving information; if you have time point these out or let him see you using them.

Make a game of spotting letters and names when you're out walking or on a car journey.

Read out where the bus is going from the sign on its front.

Point out that L stands for learner driver when you see it on a car.

Let him help you to use recipes in the kitchen, or make shopping lists.

Encourage him to read the menu with you in a restaurant.

Point out the cleaning instructions on labels in clothes or cooking

instructions on tins or frozen foods.

Read suitable excerpts from the newspaper as you are reading it. Keep a diary together.

Above all, **read stories** to him and with him. Our innate human curiosity makes us love a story and this will show that reading can be pleasurable too. As well as the usual storybooks about everyday things read fairy stories and poems. It doesn't matter if he doesn't understand every word. He will enjoy the flow and rhythm of the words.

Use his curiosity in things around him: go and look up information together from a book. Most children's libraries have a wide range of non-fiction books for very young children which will not only help you to answer his questions but also teach him one of the purposes of a library.

You'll probably be able to think of many more situations to reinforce the purpose of reading and writing and link them with speaking. Talking to your child and really listening as he replies, underlines the point of communication. He will also pick up the way words are put together, which will be a great help when he starts to sort out words on paper, and will give him a wider vocabulary and understanding of words and their purpose.

Teaching the purpose of reading should come before any teaching of letters, sounds or rules. If children are taught letters and rules parrot fashion too soon there is a danger that they will think of words and reading as being some sort of ritual and nothing to do with interesting activities. They may try initially to please adults but may label reading and writing as dull and boring.

MAKE IT FUN
3

Reading should be enjoyable. Everybody loves a story so reading stories to him and with him will associate books with pleasure: of course a nightly bedtime story is an ideal demonstration of this. Find a quiet corner where you can be comfortable together. Stop and chat about the characters and the pictures. What clues does the title give about the story? Be detectives looking for clues from the book. What will happen next? Use the words in the book to help make clear the meaning.

Vary the story reading by letting him join in with familiar words which are often repeated. He will feel more involved and feel that he is doing his bit. There is no harm in him 'reading' from memory at this stage. It will boost his confidence. Encourage him to have a go at words by stopping and leaving him to fill the gap.

Another useful bridge between reading the story to him and his reading to you is **reading aloud together.** It can be fun, especially if you put in all the different voices and special sound effects and as he makes progress you can soft pedal and gradually let him take over.

Don't make the sessions too serious. Joking with words and playing with rhymes and rhythms help to associate words with fun rather than dullness. Nursery rhymes and poems and, later, limericks are invaluable

here. Make up some yourselves!

Your local children's library is an excellent source of books for reading aloud or bedtime stories and as he begins to pick out words and read for himself you can help him choose books for him to read on his own, books which are well presented, well illustrated, with clear simple text on a subject which will appeal to him. Books with not too many pages are best to start with to give the child a sense of achievement as he finishes the book more quickly.

If you are buying books don't buy the basic reading book he is 'on' at school; rather, have a word with his teacher, and depending on the policy of the school, she may be pleased for him to take his reading book home for extra help, marking on a card how much he has read to you each time. She may be unhappy with the idea though, if only for the reason that the book could be forgotten sometimes and not be available for continuing work at school. Supplementary readers, ie. parallel readers to the graded series of reading books, and of similar difficulty, could be used.

Learning to read should be closely linked with writing. They are both for communicating, being different sides of the same coin. Get him to re-tell a familiar story to you and write each word down in clear print as he speaks. It will be most help if you write each letter accurately (see 'How the letters are made') as he will be learning from the way you write.

Get him to trace or copy the words and then read them back to you.

It would help even further if a typescript was then made. He would have a special interest in his own 'print.'

Make a looseleaf book of his work. He could write about anything he is specially interested in, eg. cars, animals, space, ballet, with illustrations if he wants to. This develops reading and writing and storywork together and gives all three more purpose. Buy or make a folder of thin card and add each page as he writes and draws. He can decorate and colour the cover to make it look bright and exciting. To begin with you could write the words he wants to say and then he could copy them, but gradually he will write more and more for himself.

ENCOURAGE ATTENTION

4

Lack of attention is a bad habit. One very common reason for problems with reading is an inability to concentrate for any length of time. T.V. encourages superficial looking and one of its dangers is that too much viewing can reduce the ability to concentrate on things which require more effort. Too much T.V. or use of the video also takes away any incentive for reading stories; it's easier to flick a switch. But reading gives independence. Children are naturally alert and curious but like adults they can be overwhelmed by **too many things demanding their attention,** bringing restlessness or lack of concentration or lethargy. This is why, when you read together, it is important to **find a quiet place** where there won't be too many distractions and where both of you can be quite still. If there is more than one child needing help choose a time when the other is asleep or occupied, if possible, as it is

usually better to give one child your full attention. Two children together, reading, has its pros and cons. They could compete with each other and thereby inspire each other to greater things or one could become dominant and make the other feel less confident and likely to give up without trying. A lot depends on the age difference and the personalities of the children involved.

Develop the ability to be still in other ways.

Look out of the window and watch the birds together, emphasising stillness and silence so that they won't fly away.

Try sitting together without any books, before you read, just sitting and looking around — it probably won't last for very long! but it will be calming for you both and concentrates the mind for the next activity.

Look for other ways to encourage habits of observation and discernment. These are natural in young children and very necessary for acquiring reading skills, to recognise and make sense of the strange shapes on the page.

Play games to stimulate observation, while car travelling, spotting letters/words in the streets, or counting up specific items eg. letter boxes, telephone boxes, birds or animals.

Play games to assist concentration, such as Snap, Pelmanism, Kim's Game (see Pre-reading Activities.)

Encourage him to **Listen to the sound of his own voice.** He must listen if he is to understand what he reads. Make a tape recording of him speaking and then of him reading.

Encourage him to **say the sounds** in the words as he writes. This makes use of his auditory memory.

Of course, a **good night's sleep** will give him a headstart in concentration for the next day. Children who yawn and droop at school are not in the best state to attend.

Don't pressurise him too much. If he finds it all too difficult his attention will quickly decrease. Little and often is much better than one long session infrequently.

Try and use his natural curiosity to decode and find out the words. If he really wants to find out he'll concentrate all right!

DEVELOP DISCRIMINATION

5

To begin with, letters look like a jumble of lines and circles and careful observation and listening is needed to discriminate between them.

You can help to develop these 'auditory and visual perception' skills from a very early age.

By drawing attention to details of shape and size as you do things together he will begin to look for himself.

He will enjoy finding letter shapes in everyday things, eg. the chains on a swing are like an 'O', its diagonal supports are like an 'A'. This all

helps to develop discrimination and observation of detail.

Some letters give rise to confusion, in particular 'p' 'b' and 'd' are often muddled and it helps to have some ways to remember them. The word 'bed' is often used to give a pictorial reminder. The two straight bits being the head and foot of the bed and the two round bits contained between them.

Work out together how letters can be remembered; eg. 's' looks like a snake. He'll probably have some good ideas. This can be linked with the previous activity.

Sequencing — ie. understanding the correct order of events in an activity is a valuable aid in the development of language and logical thinking, providing structure in written work.

Draw a simple picture for each stage of a well known activity eg. getting up in the morning, then mix up the order of the pictures and get him to put them back into the correct sequence again.

Give him a job to do, breaking it down into stages and giving a clear instruction for each stage so that he has time to understand and feel in control and doesn't get overwhelmed or flustered.

Encourage him to give you instructions or to explain to another child how something is done.

Ask him to tell you about his day at school, a party he has been to, etc. getting him to give you the correct order of events. There are many

games and activities for developing discrimination (see 'Pre-reading Activities'.)

Practise putting things into categories, sorting and assessing common links. eg.

Sort out a tin of buttons into piles of colours/sizes.

Tidy a drawer and let him help you to organise items into categories.

Help him to organise himself and develop a tidy mind eg. by putting toys away in the correct place.

Give him the job of setting the table, putting the cutlery, mats, etc. in the right places, or putting cups and saucers away for you.

It will help his reading if he makes **correct sounds** as he speaks. eg. if he says 'I must of dropped it,' instead of 'I must have dropped it' he will have difficulty making sense of what he reads. This habit is difficult to lose once it becomes established in speech and many older children still retain it in otherwise excellent written work.

PRACTISE!
PRACTISE!
PRACTISE!

6

To improve anything we need to practise. **Make it regular.** Children like an appointed time of day for doing things and will more readily agree to a pre-arranged commitment, even if otherwise they would rather be playing. That doesn't ever rule out an impromptu curl up together with a book, of course.

Choose a suitable time ie. when he is not too tired and yet not too boisterous and bursting with energy, needing more active pursuits, nor when his favourite T.V. programme is due.

When reading a story aloud put your finger under each word as you read along the line. This helps to link your speaking with the words on the page and also reinforces the habit of left to right. Left to right movement in reading is something which we in the West take for granted but it doesn't come naturally and help is needed to discipline the eyes. He will find the finger under the word useful initially when he reads aloud to you.

A bookmark is useful, apart from the obvious purpose of keeping the place it can be used to cover up lines below the one being read so that the eye doesn't wander and become confused. If there is a real problem with confusing the lines then **a masking card** could be made with a slit wide enough to see one line at a time. Use the bookmark also to write down which page he has read to and on which day so that he can see what progress he has made. Write down on the bookmark any words/sounds he consistently finds difficult or cannot read. (Not too many to begin with. Don't put down every little mistake he makes — this could be too discouraging.)

When he first starts to read he will probably be recognising words by the way they look on the page — the shape they make. This is referred to as the **Look and Say** method and he may build up a good stock of words that he can recognise just by looking. But obviously, to learn every word he will ever need is not feasible and so he will need to build up a **knowledge of phonics** eg. the sounds and sound combinations that letters make. (see Phonics list). This will help him to decipher words as he comes to them. However, there are some basic words which are irregular in spelling and not decipherable by phonic methods, so it is useful to work on learning these by the use of flash cards. (see 'Activities with letters and words'.)

Don't prompt him too quickly because by having a go he will learn how to work out an unfamiliar word — either by using his knowledge of phonics or by the position of the word in the sentence or by looking at the pictures for clues. If you always tell him he will just wait for you to say the word.

On the other hand, **don't leave him struggling** for too long or sitting in painful silence. If he is stuck, **give him clues** eg.

Look at the beginning of the word.

Look together for familiar letters or phonic groups.

Look at the picture.

Look at the words around

If he is still unsure point to the first letter and suggest its sound slightly with your lips.

Reading and writing go hand in hand so use any opportunity for him to write. Practice in writing the letters will help to familiarise him with them on the pages of a book. (see 'How the letters are made'.) Get him to practise saying the sounds they make as he writes.

The letters. Each letter has its name and the sound/s it makes — on its own or combined with other letters. The name is what it is called in the alphabet.

Each letter can be written in capital letters — ABC
Or small (lower case) letters — abc.

Use every opportunity to link reading and writing with speaking and let them be seen as a means of making contact with people, eg.

Write a note for the milkman.

Make a list of jobs to be done.

Write down ideas for birthday or Christmas presents.

Write thank you letters.

Ideally, practise **once a day.** This is much better than one long session which can be tiring for both of you. It is important that it should be something to look forward to, not a dreary session, dutifully done.

Some children find that their sense of touch can be a help in remembering letters. Get him to trace a letter or word in the air or in sand, or play 'I draw a letter on your back.' You have to guess which one he has drawn.

Make a set of 'feely' letters by cutting letter shapes from textured material. This is useful for letters which are often mixed up visually like 'b' and 'd' and 'p' and can be useful also for words which are sometimes read back to front like 'was' for 'saw' and 'no' for 'on'.

BUILD UP CONFIDENCE

7

Make reading time an occasion when he expects to succeed, and he usually will, if you're not too impatient, and bear in mind that different children learn to read at different ages. If a child has found reading difficult and needs his confidence boosting it is better to **start him on an easier book** to promote a belief in his own abilities. If he has already labelled himself (or been labelled) as no good at reading, his confidence in his own ability will probably need building up. From now on, he can start to succeed, with attention, persistence and practice.

It is important to make the **emphasis on praise** rather than criticism. Reassure him with 'good' if he attempts a word and gets it right. Look for the things he **can do** rather than those he can't. That's not to say that all the mistakes or wrong ideas should be ignored. Point them out in a matter of fact way, or guide him to tell you when correction is needed. Get him to refer to the picture or to the general sense of the story — 'Is that right?' 'What do you think?' It's not very confidence boosting to be constantly pulled up for every little mistake you make, to feel that you've done it all wrong again, but of course excess praise becomes meaningless and is seen as such by the child.

Tighten up what you expect of him as he makes progress.

Success breeds success and if he feels that he's doing O.K. he'll probably concentrate more so as not to spoil things by making mistakes. If he feels that it's all too difficult and he's afraid of failing then his attention will decrease and he will lose interest.

If he regards it as drudgery he won't make much effort, so a book about something he is really interested in, will help, as will making a book of his own.

An older child is usually very conscious of the level and type of book he is reading. He hates anything that looks too babyish and will often make out that he can read huge books of close print far beyond his capacity, to soothe his pride. A child who is finding reading difficult is usually sensitive about it, but sometimes he may adopt a cocky casual attitude, pretending that he knows all the answers, hardly realising himself that he is trying to cover up his deficiencies. It may be useful to jolt him into a realisation that he really can't do as well as he makes out, because until he realises this and is prepared to admit it to himself you won't get very far — but back this up with words of assurance that he is capable of better things. Never laugh or show horror at his mistakes; he may be too shy to try again. Only laugh with him, which unites rather than destroys.

CONCLUSION

It's a good thing to remember that children become 'reading ready' at different ages so **don't expect too much too soon.**

Don't try too hard or pressurise him too much, especially if he is still very young. It may end up by working the opposite way; you could kill enjoyment and make him hate reading and associate books with slog rather than with pleasurable activity.

This doesn't mean that you sit back and wait for him to show an interest in words. He may never do that, left to his own devices.

You're there to guide him and to show him how to learn and find out. The word **'educate'** comes from the latin **'educere'** which means 'to lead or draw out'.

Work together to learn. You may find that you learn something too, not least a greater understanding of how he thinks and learns.

There is no set way to teach. Fit reading to the child, not the child to reading.

Use your imagination to think of new ways of getting him to understand about words and reading. This is where parents can do such a valuable job, by channelling the child's interest and making his path to reading an easy and enjoyable one, encouraging habits of observation and discernment which are natural in young children and very necessary for acquiring the skills of reading.

If progress is slow don't worry unnecessarily; worry can be infectious and he may become anxious too. Try to keep him interested in reading and as likely as not he'll suddenly take off.

ACTIVITIES AND BOOKLIST

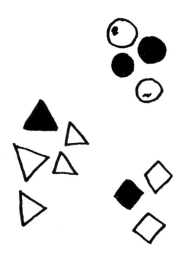

PRE-READING ACTIVITIES

Practice in discriminating shapes, colours etc.

Sort out a tin of buttons into piles of colours/sizes.

Tidy a drawer and let him help to organise items into categories.

Help him to organise himself and develop a tidy mind eg. by putting toys away in their correct place.

Give him the job of setting the table, putting the cutlery, mats etc. in the right places, or putting plates, cups and saucers away.

Games to buy

My First Pairs (Ladybird)

My First Dominoes (Ladybird)

This Way, That Way Matching shapes and pictures (Nathan Games)

Railway Snap   Michael Stanfield

'Same or Different' colour cards Taskmaster DLM175
(30 cards featuring pairs of 15 different items which stress colour differences and likeness)

Visual Discrimination Activity Booklets, set of two
(Learning Development Aids) LD344

Classification LDA LD19
(30 cards — each object can be classified according to group and size.)

'What's Wrong' cards L.D.A. LD50
(30 cards. In identifying and explaining the absurdities the child is developing his conceptual thinking skills.)

Spell and Learn Early Learning Centre
Identify the letters and join them to the correct picture. Helps learning to spell. 28 pictures and 56 letter pieces.

Alphabet Game Early Learning Centre
A simple game to help recognition of the alphabet.
52 picture and letter pieces.

Picture Word Dominoes Galt Toys
Match the words to the pictures in this colourful game of dominoes that can greatly assist in word building and vocabulary development.

Fun to Write Galt Toys
Step by Step guide to writing and learning letters.

Letter Stencils Early Learning Centre
26 stencil tablets with illustrated guide.

Picture Word Cards Early Learning Centre
Match the 40 word cards with the 40 picture cards. Only the correct card will fit. Helps word recognition.

Magnetic Spelling Board Early Learning Centre
40 letters and magnetic board.

Stack 'n Rock Early Learning Centre
Colour matching and grading. Stack the seven rainbow coloured rings into a rocking base in size and colour order.

Shapes Game   Galt Toys
A fun game to encourage shape and colour recognition.

Cover Match   Galt Toys
Cover up as many matching symbols as you can. Colour and shape matching game for up to six players.

Posting Box   Early Learning Centre
A simple first posting box with six shapes to post.

Mighty Mind   Spears Games
32 colourful wooden design tiles in 6 geometric shapes which are matched to and then fit over pictures on 30 design pattern cards of increasing difficulty.

Play and Learn   Young Explorers
Colour and shape set. Shape, size and colour recognition and discrimination, developing language skills, creative and logical thinking, manual dexterity.

Shape Sorter   Mothercare
Posting basket with carry handle, lift up lid and four play tools. Encourages recognition of shape at an early age. Designed to teach co-ordination.

Lotto. A simple game of picture recognition to help develop matching and language skills. Contains 4 colourful playing boards and 24 playing pieces.

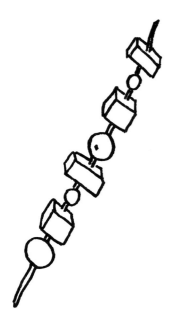

Practice in sequencing and placing in correct order.

Draw or cut out a series of pictures, each illustrating a stage in a familiar activity eg. getting up in the morning. Ask him to put them in the correct order of happening.

Thread beads in a simple pattern and ask him to repeat the pattern eg. red/blue/green/yellow.

Games to buy

Sequential picture cards   Taskmaster DLM 161
(Ideal for beginning practice in sequencing.)

Visual recall flash cards   L.D.A. LD91
(The ability to recall sequences is crucial for language and reading development.)

Sequential thinking cards   L.D.A. LD9 LD13 LD14
(30 cards — sets of sequences which become longer and more complex.)

Sequencing beads   Taskmaster DLM289
(four geometric shapes each in three sizes. Five colours, threading laces included.)

Sequencing bead patterns   Taskmaster DLM290

Sizing cards   Taskmaster DLM161

Assist powers of concentration through listening and looking.
'Kim's game' A number of familiar objects are placed on a tray

eg. pencil, rubber, toy car, elastic band, safety pin. Start with a small number and increase as he improves. The object of the game is to remember all the items on the tray after they have been removed from the room.

'The listening game' Read a story or piece of information. When a pre-arranged sound eg. 'sh' comes up in the reading the child must clap his hands. Choose any sounds which you feel he needs to practise.

'I went to the shops' One of you begins by saying; 'I went to the shops and I bought a . . . choosing a common object eg. a packet of biscuits. You then take it in turns to 'buy something' until there is a long list of things to remember, as each item must be mentioned each time it's your turn.

'Pelmanism' You need a pack of cards which contains at least two of every picture (a pack of snap cards will do) The cards are turned face down and the players take it in turns to turn over two cards. The object of the game is to turn over two which are identical, and win as many pairs as possible. This requires careful observation of the position of each card as they mustn't be moved out of place. This could also be played using two sets of alphabet cards (one capitals, one lower case) trying to make a pair.

Games to buy

Look Hear! L.D.A. LD125 3 C20 tapes 35 photographs
(six complete sound/picture matching exercises using sounds and

attractive colour photographs. Each game takes a theme.)

1. Human sounds 2. Daily sounds 3. Home sounds
4. School sounds 5. Transport sounds 6. Animal sounds

Wotami? (What am I?) L.D.A. LD 336
There are sixteen songs on this stereo cassette, each about a living thing which is never mentioned by name. Words and music provide clues to help the listener identify each one.

ACTIVITIES WITH LETTERS AND WORDS

Practice in use of letters/sounds

Games to make. 5 finger puppets with a vowel on each one. Use an old glove, making each finger/thumb into a different character and embroider on it the appropriate letters. a, e, i, o, u. You read a three letter word eg. 'big' (i) or 'hot' (o) and he wriggles the correct finger when he hears the sound of the vowel.

brick | brown
brim
brake | bright
brush

Wishing well For practising the 'sh' sound. A cardboard box is used for the well. Paint it with a brick pattern if you like. Write words with the 'sh' sound in them eg. fish, dish, shop, on small pieces of paper to which a paper clip is attached and put them in the well. Using a stick with a magnet attached to it the players take it in turns to 'fish' out a word. If they can read the word they get a point. The one with most points wins.

Brick wall Draw a wall and get him to fill in each brick with 'br' words. Or draw a row of bottles and ask him to fill each bottle with words which have 'tt' in them.

'I spy' Players take it in turn to choose something which they can see at that moment, telling the others the sound or letter it begins with. The others have to guess the chosen object.

Magic coin game Real or pretend shopping. He can buy anything beginning with the same letter/sound as his own name.

Dig for treasure Put alphabet letters (or any letters from a word games eg. scrabble, lexicon) into a drawstring bag or a box. Players take out six letters each and try to make a word/words from a given list. Each time a player uses a letter he takes another from the bag. The winner is the one with most letters used.

Practice in word recognition

Give instructions for finding something interesting eg. a toy or food by simple Look and Say flash card sentences.

Place name cards around the house, labelling common articles.

Make a word list of all the words he knows as they come up and keep adding to it to see how long it can get.

Jigsaw Write words on cards and cut up into syllables. (A useful guide as to how many syllables there are in a word is to place the hand under the chin and say the word distinctly eg. ba/na/na counting the number of times your hand moves) Ask him to try and fit the word together again.

Use a cassette recorder. He will often self correct his own reading when he plays it back.

Word Snap. Use a set of flash cards ie. cards with one word printed clearly on each card. Make your own, choosing words which should be familiar, or buy a set of Ladybird flash cards.

The cards are divided equally among the players, who take turns to turn over the cards. When two identical cards are turned over the first player to shout the word out picks up all the cards. The winner is the one who gets all the cards or the most cards at the end of a given time.

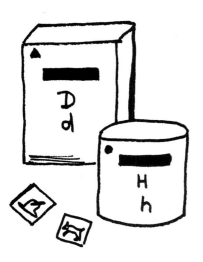

Postboxes. Make a number of postboxes out of old cereal packets or any carton or container by cutting a slot in each one. Print a different letter on each one in capitals and lower case. eg. A a.

Make a collection of pictures of well known objects, either draw them yourself or cut from magazines, which have initial letters corresponding to the letters on your postboxes. On the back of each picture mark all those beginning with the same letter with the same symbol eg. A triangle on all those beginning with D. Likewise mark the appropriate box. When all the pictures are posted the child can check for himself by using the symbols on the reverse of the picture and on the box.

Simon Says. A word version of the well known game using flash cards to give instructions like 'hop' 'skip' etc. The child has to obey the instructions on the card.

Pick an Apple. Draw a giant apple tree. Cut it out and pin it on the wall/door. On each branch stick paper apple shapes on which are written words from a particular word family. eg. 'bat', 'rat', 'cat', 'fat', 'sat' or 'look', 'cook', 'rook', 'took'. Use words which will occur in the books he reads to you. Get him to help you write the word.

As he reads aloud to you and recognises a word on the 'apple tree' he can take it from the tree and put it into an envelope until he has a 'branchful' when he can be rewarded with a real apple!

Phonic Dominoes. Make a set of dominoes with words instead of dots. Choose words from word families with the same phonic sounds. eg. g<u>oa</u>t, b<u>oa</u>t, fl<u>oa</u>t, or f<u>ee</u>t, m<u>ee</u>t, k<u>ee</u>p, or p<u>a</u>ne, m<u>a</u>ne, f<u>a</u>de.

The players start with seven dominoes each. The remainder are placed face down in the centre. Throw a die to decide who starts. Each player has to place one of his dominoes with the same sound as the underlined part of the preceding domino. If he can't go then he has to take a domino from the centre pile. The first one to get rid of all his dominoes is the winner.

'Feet' words. Draw round the child's foot and see how many 'ee' words you can fit on the foot shape.

Roller Words. On one half of a toilet roll rube write consonants or initial blends eg. 'tr', 'bl', 'sp', and on a large kitchen roll tube write a word part eg. 'ot'. The short tube is placed over the end of the large tube and is turned round, making several different words which the child reads out. Make several 'rollers' with different letter combinations.

Bingo. A version of the well known game using letter or sound combinations. The child has a card with a selection of letters/sounds written on it and a pile of counters or cardboard squares. You have a selection of letters/sounds written on small cardboard squares in a container from which you choose randomly and call out the sound (not the name of the letter). The child must cover the letter if he has it on his card. Match up the ones he has covered with the cardboard squares you have taken out, when he has filled his card.

Make one or two cards to begin with and when the letters/sounds have been practised, introduce more complex phonic combinations.

Find the Word. Place a number of small items eg. pencil, penny, ribbon, button etc. in a large envelope. The names of the articles are printed on the envelope. Each item must be placed against its name. Choose easy words to begin with, then move on to more difficult ones.

Spin a Word. Cut a regular hexagon shape out of card and print a word on each of the six edges. Put a stick or a pencil through the centre of the card. The child spins the card and when it stops he reads the word nearest to him.

Sorting. A selection of words are printed on small cards. eg. 'hat', 'dog', 'shoe', 'cat' and the child sorts them under separate headings eg. 'things we wear' 'pets' etc. Choose words from the book you are reading at the moment.

Matchboxes. Cut out small pictures of everyday things and write their names on separate pieces of paper. Make a collection of different shaped small boxes or containers and place a picture inside each one. Stick the appropriate name on the outside. The child opens the box to find out what the word is. After a while he will be able to read the word without opening the box.

Sound Snap. Use a set of lexicon cards or any other similar letter game. Spread a number of the cards out and make the sound of the letter. The child has to pick up the letter matching the sound you have made. Start with a few and increase the number as he makes progress.

Games to buy

Flexi cling letters (lower case)   Boots (Chemist)
(cling onto shiny surfaces eg. windows, mirrors).

Rhyming cards   Taskmaster DLM 235

Brogy   Taskmaster T 570
(210 plastic cards for improving reading, writing and spelling)

Sounds Fun   L.D.A. LD 102
(41 phonetically based poems. Each poem concentrates on one sound.)

Phonic blend dominoes L.D.A. LD 2411 108 dominoes

The Bron word builder L.D.A. LD 346
(A reading machine made from strong plastic)

'Make a badge'   John Adams Toys
(blank badges and lettering.)

Lift and Look playtray   Early Learning Centre
(questions link words with activity)

Phonic fish   Cambridge Educational 6 packs
(each pack deals with a selection of sounds)

Irregularly spelt words cannot be deciphered using phonics, so it is
useful to learn them by **Look and Say.** Use the words in games eg.
Pelmanism or make your own flash cards. Write one word to a card, just
a few cards to begin with, increasing as he becomes more proficient.
Look at each word together, saying what it is, trying to find ways of

remembering its shape. eg. sticks in the air or downwards, does anything link with what the word means eg. 'look' has 'two eyes'. Then hold each card briefly in front of the child for him to say what it is.

Some of the most common irregularly spelt words.

was	all	are	have	one	said	come	some	more
before	do	they	two	were	your	who	what	could
would	any	many	girl	you	walk	talk	work	because
front	here	enough	sure	father	mother	first	water	watch
once	friend	our	want	the	little	their	where	blue

BOOKLIST

Many of the following are published with teachers in mind, for use in schools.

Ideas books

Bright Ideas for Reading Activities
Scholastic Publications Ltd.

Phonics Resource Bank and Teachers' guide
Jill Gregory   Pub. John Murray

Work books

All Round English (series)
R. Ridout   Pub. Longman

Starting with Words — introductory workbook of above series
(A carefully graded course in language.)

Ladybird Workbooks
Learn to Write, Learning to Read. Learning the Alphabet.
Read, Write and Remember
Constance Milburn   Pub. Blackie
Pre-reading Activity Books (four graded workbooks)
Jenny Ackland   Pub. Oxford U.P.
Sounds of Words bks. 1 & 2 Robert Gibson (pub)
Sounding & Blending 5 books a e i o u Robert Gibson
Picture Words   R. Ridout Dragon Puzzle Books

Reading books

Read along Stories   Cambridge Ed. Set 1 (six books)
(Designed to be read by beginning readers and adults together or later
by children on their own).
Fuzzbuzz   Oxford U.P. Pk. of six books
(carefully structured readers with plenty of repetition)
Puddle Lane Reading Programme   Sheila McCullagh   Ladybird
An excellent graded series of books, also Puddle Lane frieze,
word cards, jigsaws, cassettes, picture dominoes and activity books.
Dragon Pirate books
Griffin Pirate books   Sheila McCullagh
I unpacked My Grandmother's Trunk   Susan Ramsay Houet
(a book that can be used as a memory game/teaching the alphabet)
Oxford U.P.

Best Word Book Ever   Richard Scarry   Hamlyn
Oxford Picture Word Book   O.U.P.

Cassettes

'Read-along' book and tape (series) Rainbow Communications Ltd.
(Star Trek, E.T. Star Wars etc.)
Flying Start
(A reading scheme which includes selected readings on tapes, and
puzzle books with words and pictures. Level 1 features the book 'Picture
Words' with emphasis on word and picture matching and includes many
exercises dealing with initial letter names and sounds and short vowels.
The child is given a great deal of support to get him off to a good and
confident start.

T.V. Programmes: B.B.C. 'Words and Pictures' 'Look and Read'.

PHONICS
LETTERS AND SOUNDS

Learning phonics provides an important key to fluent and
independent reading.

The 26 letters of the alphabet are divided into vowels and consonants.

The Vowels   **a e i o u** each have two sounds.

The short sound
a as in at   **e** as in hen   **i** as in bit
o as in cod   **u** as in cub

The long sound. (the name of the vowel) made by adding an e to the word.

a as in ate   **e** as in these   **i** as in bite
o as in code   **u** as in cube

The consonants (don't add a vowel as you make the sound)

b as in bat	**d** as in dip	**f** as in fish	**h** as in hot
j as in jump	**k** as in kettle	**l** as in lip	**m** as in mat
n as in net	**p** as in pig	**r** as in rat	**t** as in tap
v as in van	**w** as in wig	**x** as in fox	**z** as in zebra

c has two sounds   **g** has two sounds

    c as in cat   **g** as in goat
    c as in cell   **g** as in giant

s has two sounds

    s as in sat
    s as in please

y has three sounds

    y as in yes
    y as in slowly } here making the two i sounds
    y as in fly

Vowel combinations

ai as in rain
au as in autumn
ea as in tea,   as in head,   as in break,   as in early
ei as in eight

ie as in field
ee as in meet
oa as in coal
oe as in toe
oi as in coin
oo as in moon,   as in wood,   as in door
ou as in touch,   as in soup,   as in cloud
ui as in build,   as in disguise
ua as in guard
ue as in guess

Consonant combinations

ck as in clock	**sh** as in shell	**st** as in stone
sp as in spell	**tr** as in trap	**cr** as in cream
ch as in church	**ch** as in ache	**ch** as in chute
sc as in scream	**sk** as in skip	**sl** as in slip
sw as in swim	**pl** as in play	**pr** as in prim
sm as in smear	**sn** as in snail	**tw** as in twist
fr as in frost	**gl** as in glass	**wh** as in where
ph as in photograph		

Double consonants
pp dd nn tt rr gg zz ll ff bb ss

Vowel and consonant combinations
ar as in bar,   as in care,   as in war,   as in sugar,   as in carry
aw as in saw
ay as in play
er as in other
ir as in bird
ow as in cow, as in barrow
or as in story, as in word
oy as in boy
ur sounding like ir as in turn

Silent letters
w k b h u c g n o l

Word endings
y s es ing ed le nd mp nk ang ong ung ture tion sion ous ious fle gle ple tle ight.

Alteration of sound
g sounding like **j** as in bridge   **c** sounding like **sh** as in ocean
s sounding like **sh** as in sugar   **c** sounding like **s** as in cigarette

HOW THE SMALL LETTERS ARE MADE

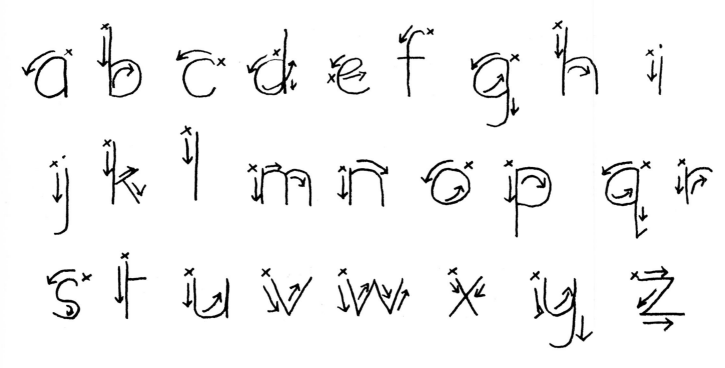

Begin to make the letter at the cross

HOW THE CAPITALS ARE MADE

ADDRESSES OF EDUCATIONAL SUPPLIERS

Learning Development Aids
Duke Street
Wisbech
Cambs. PE13 2AE
Tel: (0945) 63441

Taskmaster Ltd.
Morris Road
Leicester LE2 6BR
Tel: 0533 704286

Scholastic Publications Ltd.
Westfield Road
Southam
Leamington Spa
Warwickshire CV33 0JH
Tel: 092 681 3910

Robert Gibson
17 Fitzroy Place
Glasgow G3 7BR
Tel: 041 248 5674

Cambridge University Press
The Edinburgh Building
Shasftesbury Road
Cambridge CB2 2RU
Tel: (0223) 312393

Ginn & Co.
Elsinore House,
Buckingham Street,
Aylesbury
Bucks.

'Flying Start'
54, Beresford Avenue
Tolworth
Surbiton
Surrey KT5 9LJ
Tel: 01-390 2975

BOOK CLUBS

As at your school about Book Clubs. Many schools run them now and they offer a good range of fact and fiction books for children at a reduced price and are an excellent way to encourage book ownership and reading.

Book Club for Parents.

Books for Children
PO Box 50,
Leicestershire LE1 9AW   Tel: 0858 410 510

Offers a wide range of hardback books chosen by experts for children of all ages, at substantially less than the publishers' prices.

Organisations which give advice on children's books.

The National Book League,
Children's Book Centre,
Book House,
45 East Hill,
London SW18 2QZ   Tel: 01-870 9055

They will supply booklists and publications and are a useful source of information about children and books.

The Booksellers' Association of Great Britain and Ireland,
154 Buckingham Palace Road,
London SW1W 9TZ   Tel: 01-730 8214

They will advise where to buy children's books in your area.

REVIEWS OF CHILDREN'S BOOKS

Children's books are reviewed regularly in the Times Educational Supplement, Child Education, Junior Education and The Teacher, as well as newspapers such as the Observer, The Sunday Times and some of the daily papers.

There are also Review Journals dealing solely with children's books.

The Signal Selection of Children's Books. Published annually by Thimble Press, Lockwood, Station Road, South Woodchester, Stroud, Gloucestershire GL5 5EQ Tel: 045383 3460

Aims to identify the most interesting and important books out of a year's publishing, from baby books to novels for teenagers.

Books For Your Children. The Parents Guide. 34 Harborne Road, Edgbaston, Birmingham. Tel: 021 454 5453

A colourful, well presented magazine, three issues a year reviewing new fiction and non-fiction books for all ages and encouraging links between teachers, librarians and parents.